Rush Limbaugh

and

Noble Albino

Redwood Tree

by

Richard Mays

Illustrated

by

Darin Lucas

1.

Terror was the only companion that Albino Redwood Tree had.

His fate, it seemed, had been sealed.

Standing at a majestic height of 52 feet, it had struggled for its entire life to see the sun.

Sadly, it was never to reach 53 feet,

as a lite rail commuter train bore down on it.

2.

Only an engineer who resembled Barbara Boxer and a conductor, which for all to see, looked exactly like Nancy Pelosi, were its only riders.

For, as everyone knows, no one else would dare to ride the train of sorrow.

The ear to ear cavernous smile on Boxer's face was complimented by her squinting eyes. They were fixated on poor, quiet, Albino Redwood.

Above the rumble and roar of the government paid for and population unused train, you could hear the shrill voice of Pelosi screaming "Kill the tree! Run it down!"

The Albino Redwood had finally accepted the fact that its long years of solitude, watching mankind grow from peaceful Indian tribes to the insanity driven liberals, had now come to an end.

These are the ones that now run the state and had sealed his fate.

A small tear running down its bark was its only defense.

3.

Life had not always been so cruel to this stately, majestic denizen of the forest.

More years ago than it could even remember, a seed dropped to the ground and a miracle of nature began to grow.

Bursting through the soil, a new life had appeared. But this was not just any redwood beginning its life path, but a marvelous thing happened.

It was blessed to become a hybrid of a redwood tree and something special that would allow it to be an Albino Redwood.

It did not know it at the time, but it was to be only one of ten of its kind growing on the face of the planet.

Mankind and animal alike were both awed and humbled by this Prince of trees.

4.

Deer would lie down in circles to protect it at night. Daylight would find wolves patrolling a defensive pattern to make sure no harm would befall.

As the noble Albino Redwood continued to grow, the animals performed a tremendous job of protection.

At some point, they realized it was time to pass the task of protection onto the fearless Native American.

5.

The proud Native Americans immediately recognized the tree for what it was...a gift.

They watered it. They kept away unwanted insects. They made sure no harm was to mar this Albino Redwood. They passed their honor and trust onto each new generation who gladly shouldered this task.

But, sadly, the wolves were killed off and the graceful Native Americans were forced off of their ancestral lands.

Still, it grew. It grew tall. It grew straight. It stretched toward the life giving sun.

As time passed, it was blissfully unaware that its protective world was ebbing away.

It was blind to the great consuming threat that was claiming the land for its own nefarious purposes. This blight on the land had a name...Liberals.

6.

Just the name "Liberal" sends chills up the legs of people who love freedom.

Noble Albino Redwood did not know of such chills. It believed in the goodness of mankind as was demonstrated to it by the proud Native American.

For untold decades, it stood in reverence of these proud people.

Unlike those peace loving peoples, the liberals have only vague memories of putting the love of nature above worthless technology.

Liberals decided to build a lite rail system without regard to the unique Albino Redwood. They heartlessly chose an overpriced government machine over more than the stately, one of ten unique trees.

In their minds the reason was simple; they could not force a tree to pay taxes.

7.

They mapped the tracks path to do what no one else would have dared to do...destroy it.

In secret they plotted this vile and despicable deed. But like all evil, word eventually oozed into the daylight.

Still no one came to protect Noble Albino Redwood.

The tree killing commuter train, clawed ever closer. It wanted only the death of this ancient, unique life form.

8.

But then, it started. Soft, as a spring breeze, that gently, blows on a new born flower. Noble Albino Redwood slowly lifted its sad, tear-filled eyes, to the southeast. A tingle began to rise up its core.

Noble Albino Redwood's eyes that had been blurred by despair saw a dot on the horizon. A sound like a strong heartbeat began to grow. It came straight toward noble Albino Redwood.

Moving at high speed, it saw the dot grow to become a powerful SUV.

The sounds of the heartbeat grew to a dull rumble, and then to a ground shaking roar.

The tinted window SUV slid to a stop with a mighty snarl. The driver side door flew open and out stepped a man.

This man was unlike anyone Noble Albino Redwood had ever encountered in its long life.

9.

He was tall. He was strong. He had steely eyes that told everyone that he was a man of courage and action. He began to survey the area.

His mouth carried a grin that told Noble Albino Redwood...you have a friend in me.

Without a word, he walked straight to Noble Albino Redwood and stared at its majestic stature.

In a faint and tired voice, Noble Albino Redwood managed to croak, "Who...are...you?"

Lighting a cigar, taking a puff, he replied "I, am Rush Limbaugh and I, am at your service".

His words were like thunder that echoed in the hills and yet they were comfortingly warm in Noble Albino Redwood's core.

His voice was powerful...like freedom itself.

Before Noble Albino Redwood could react, their attention was drawn to an irritating noise coming from the commuter train.

10.

A noise, which most people, understood to be a ghastly screech. This noise always comes out of self-centered, power mad, small minded Liberals.

The noise began to be heard as a chant "Ho, Ho Hey, Hey...How many trees can we kill today?"

This is a chant that these narrow minded, bigoted people had used for decades to drive their self-serving destructive polices.

Courageous Rush knew Liberals for what they truly are...cowards, who can only gain power by spending other people's money.

When they saw Courageous Rush, a ball of fear grew in their knotted stomachs and black hearts.

They decided that the only way to assuage their fears was to destroy them both.

11.

Giving no thought for his own safety, Courageous Rush he placed himself between Noble Albino Redwood and the tree killing Liberals.

A crowd had gathered to witness the destruction of a living life form.

Courageous Rush possesses many great qualities. One of the greatest is the reverence for life in all of its forms.

He turned to the crowd and gave them the opportunity to stand up for all that is right and good in this fabled country. "Who among you will join me in saving this life?"

All of the groups who pretended to stand up for the oppressed, turned their backs on this defenseless creature. This served only to prove their hypocrisy.

They gave up all of their so-called beliefs in exchange for a bloated government project that they could not afford to build themselves.

Courageous Rush knew Liberal's convictions only run as deep as the thickness of a tree leaf. But honor commanded of him to offer them the opportunity of redemption.

Turning sideways, he put his left hand toward Noble Albino Redwood and his right hand toward the tree eating commuter train.

12.

As it bore down, the focus was taken off of Noble Albino Redwood and placed on Courageous Rush. Rush knew that Liberals hate a person who can think independently more than their love of disposing of helpless life forms.

The engineer began screaming at the top of her lungs "No one has thoughts that are not approved by us!"

Courageous Rush stood his ground and roared "Not Today!"

At the last second, he auto started his SUV and sent it in front of the death train. The impact caused a massive shatter of metal and glass. The crushed, twisted heap of modern machinery slid toward the new team of Noble Albino Redwood and Courageous Rush.

13.

He placed his back against the tree to shield it with his body. As the wreckage approached, it began to break into two streams. It flowed around both sides and formed a circle of debris.

As the carnage ground to a halt, Courageous Rush said a silent prayer to God for giving him courage and protection.

Turning, he could not care less about the now defunct train. His concern was seeing a large gash in Noble Albino Redwood's base. This was allowing its life force to stream out.

His eyes caught sight of Noble Albino Redwood's eyes. He could see its life ebbing away. The terror that the Liberals had caused, combined with the massive gash was more than Noble Albino Redwood was able to overcome.

14.

As tears streamed down Courageous Rush's face, Noble Albino Redwood said "My life is over...but you have proven to be a man of honor".

It took a labored breath and spoke these last words, "I trust you with my...only gift"

With that, Noble Albino Redwood passed to be one with its ancestors. A branch slowly opened and allowed seedlings, which it was nurturing, to fall at Courageous Rush's feet.

Courageous Rush's backbone is arrow straight and as large as a telephone pole, but he felt proud to stoop down to retrieve these gifts.

His sadness at the loss of Noble Albino Redwood was tempered by the new lives that were now his responsibility.

15.

With an armload of seedlings and a sneer for the gutless Liberals, he strode through them as if they did not exist.

Already, he was making plans on how to continue Noble Albino Redwood's legacy.

If a person is judged by leadership and compassion, surely Courageous Rush will forever be a man among men.

The End.

This unlikely, yet true story.

-

In northern California, near the small town of Cotati, stands a 52 foot tall wonder of nature. An albino redwood tree.

A tree that is so rare, it should be treated with utmost respect.

Sadly, the transportation unit know as

Sonoma-Marin Area Transit

or

"SMART"

has plans to lay its tracks so close to the tree that they feel that it must be destroyed.

A tree, that has been labeled a Scientific Treasure, was given secondary status. This is in deference to a lite rail train that refuses to alter its course even slightly.

Carolyn Glendening (the spokeswoman for SMART) said they have the authorization to go forward and they continue their path unabated.

Uncaring government officials need to learn to protect life, not destroy it.

People need to travel to Sonoma County, while they still have the chance, to see this incredible tree with their own eyes.

"Save all life" should be first and foremost in all of our minds.

Richard Mays

www.ingramcontent.com/pod-product-compliance
Lightning Source LLC
Chambersburg PA
CBHW070245290526
45789CB00004B/1770